Comedy and Tragedy

A Bibliography of Critical Studies

Comedy and Tragedy
A Bibliography of Critical Studies

by
E. H. Mikhail

The Whitston Publishing Company
Incorporated
Troy, New York
1972

CONTENTS

PREFACE

Studies of Comedy and Tragedy have recently been on the increase, and a bibliography of criticism is overdue. Checklists and selected bibliographies have appeared separately or incorporated in books and periodicals. These, however, are either selective, or deal mainly with special topics, such as "Greek Tragedy" or "Restoration Comedy". The present work, which comprises some 320 entries, is the first attempt towards a comprehensive "General" bibliography. This is not to draw attention to its completeness, but rather to ask pardon for any possible shortcomings. I have tried to make it complete until the end of the year 1970, although some late studies have been included.

The following bibliographical aids have been checked to set up the groundwork of my Bibliography:

Abstracts of English Studies, 1958 - present. Boulder, Col.: National Council of Teachers of English.

Annual Bibliography of English Language and Literature, 1920 - present. London: Modern Humanities Research Association.

Cambridge Bibliography of English Literature, 5 vols. Cambridge: Cambridge University Press.

Cumulative Book Index, 1928 - present. New York: H. W. Wilson.

Dissertation Abstracts, 1938 - present. Ann Arbor, Mich.: University Microfilms.

Dissertations in English and American Literature; Theses Accepted by American, British and German Universities, 1865–1964, by Lawrence F. McNamee. New York & London: R. R. Bowker, 1968.

Doctoral Dissertations Accepted by American Universities, ed. Arnold H. Trotier and Marian Harman. New York: H. W. Wilson, 1933–1955. Continued as *Index to American Doctoral Dissertations*, 1955 - present.

Dramatic Index, 1909–1949. Boston: F. W. Faxon.

Essay and General Literature Index, 1900 - present. New York: H. W. Wilson.

Index to Little Magazines, 1943 - present. Denver: Alan Swallow.

Index to One-Act Plays, comp. by Hannah Logasa and Winifred Ver Nooy. Boston: F. W. Faxon, 1924; *Supplement, 1924–1931*. Boston: F. W. Faxon, 1932; *Second Supplement, 1932–1940*. Boston: F. W. Faxon, 1941; *Third Supplement, 1941–1948*. Boston: F. W. Faxon, 1950; *Fourth Supplement, 1948–1957*. Boston: F. W. Faxon, 1958.

Index to Plays 1800–1926, comp. by Ina Ten Eyck Firkins. New York: H. W. Wilson, 1927.

Index to Plays; Supplement, comp. by Ina Ten Eyck Firkins.

iv

New York: H. W. Wilson, 1935.

Index to Plays in Collections, ed. John H. Ottemiller. Washington: The Scarecrow Press, 1951.

Index to Theses Accepted for Higher Degrees in the Universities of Great Britain and Ireland, 1950 - present. London: Aslib.

International Index to Periodicals, 1907 - present. New York: H. W. Wilson. From vol. 19 (April 1965—March 1966) called *Social Sciences and Humanities Index.*

Masters Abstracts, 1962 - present. Ann Arbor, Mich.: University Microfilms.

New York Times Index.

PMLA Bibliography.

Play Index 1949—1952; An Index to 2626 Plays in 1138 Volumes, comp. by Dorothy Herbert West and Dorothy Margaret Peake. New York: H. W. Wilson, 1953.

Reader's Guide to Periodical Literature, 1900 - present. New York: H. W. Wilson.

Subject Index to Periodicals, 1915—1961. London: The Library Association. Continued as *British Humanities Index*, 1962 - present.

Theatre Dissertations, ed. Frederic M. Little. Kent: Kent State University Press, 1969.

The Times Index.

Year's Work in English Studies, 1919 - present. London:
The English Association.

E. H. MIKHAIL

London, May 1971

A BIBLIOGRAPHY OF CRITICAL STUDIES

Comedy

A Bibliography of Critical Studies

(a) Books

Aikin-Sneath, Betsy. *Comedy in Germany in the First Half of the Eighteenth Century.* Oxford: Clarendon Press, 1936.

Aristotle. *Poetics.*

Aubouin, Elie. *Technique et psychologie du comique.* Paris: 1948.

Bahnsen, Julius. *Das Tragische und der Humor.* Leipzig: J. A. Barth, 1931.

Baudelaire, Charles. "On the Essence of Laughter" [1855], *The Mirror of Art,* trans. and ed. Jonathan Mayne. London: Phaidon Press, 1955.

Beattie, James. "Essay on Laughter and Ludicrous Composition," *Essays.* Edinburgh: William Creech, 1776.

Beerbohm, Max. "The Humour of the Public," *Yet Again.* London: Chapman & Hall, 1909.

-- "Laughter," *And Even Now.* New York: E. P. Dutton, 1921.

Behrman, S. N. "What Makes Comedy High?" *American Playwrights on Drama,* ed. Horst Frenz. New York:

Hill & Wang, 1965. Reprinted from *New York Times* (30 March 1952), Section 2, p. 1.

Bentley, Eric. "The Psychology of Farce," *Let's Get a Divorce! And Other Plays*. New York: Mermaid Dramabook, 1958.

Bergler, Edmund. *Laughter and the Sense of Humor*. New York: International Medical Book Corporation, 1956.

Bergson, Henri. *Laughter; An Essay on the Meaning of the Comic*, trans. by C. Brereton and F. Rothwell. London: Macmillan, 1921.

Blair, Walter, ed. *Native American Humour 1800—1900*. New York: American Book, 1937.

Blistein, Elmer M. *Comedy in Action*. Durham, N.C.: Duke University Press, 1964.

Brereton, G. "Comedy," *Cassell's Encyclopaedia of Literature*, vol. 1. London: Cassell, 1953.

Butler, Samuel. *The Humour of Homer and Other Essays*. London: Fifield, 1913.

Buxton, C. R. "What Is Comedy?" *A Politician Plays Truant: Essays on English Literature*. London: Christophers, 1929.

Campbell, Joseph. "Tragedy and Comedy," *The Hero with a Thousand Faces*. Bellingen Series XVII. New York: Pantheon Books, 1949.

Cannon, Gilbert. *Satire*. New York: 1915.

Chesterton, G. K. "On the Comic Spirit," *Eight Great Comedies*, ed. Sylvan Barnet, Morton Berman and William Burto. New York: Mentor Books, 1958.

Congreve, William. *Concerning Humour in Comedy*, 2 vols. London: S. Crowder, C. Ware & T. Payne, 1773.

Cook, Albert S. *The Dark Voyage and the Golden Mean; A Philosophy of Comedy*. Cambridge, Mass.: Harvard University Press, 1949.

Cooper, Lane. *An Aristotelian Theory of Comedy*. New York: Harcourt, Brace, 1922.

Cornford, Francis Macdonald. *The Origin of Attic Comedy*. Cambridge: Cambridge University Press, 1934.

Corrigan, Robert W., ed. *Comedy: Meaning and Form*. San Francisco: Chandler, 1965.

Courdaveaux, Victor. *Etudes sur le comique: Le rire dans la vie et dans l'art*. Paris: Librairie académique, 1875.

Courtney, W. L. "The Idea of Comedy," *Old Saws and Modern Instances*. London: Chapman & Hall, 1918. Reprinted from *Fortnightly Review*, XCV, New Series

(May 1914), 843—858.

Darlington, W. A. *Through the Fourth Wall*. London: Chapman & Hall, 1922.

Darwin, Charles. *The Expression of the Emotions in Man and Animals* [1872], ed. Francis Darwin. London: John Murray, 1904.

Dobrée, Bonamy. "Comedy," *Eight Great Comedies*, ed. Sylvan Barnet, Morton Berman and William Burton. New York: Mentor Books, 1958.

Donaldson, Ian. *The World Upside-Down: Comedy from Jonson to Fielding*. London: Oxford University Press, 1970.

Drew, Elizabeth. "Comedy," *Discovering Drama*. New York: W. W. Norton; London: Jonathan Cape, 1937.

Dugas, L. *Psychologie du rire*. Paris: Ancienne Librairie Germer Baillière, 1902.

Dumont, Léon. *Des Causes du rire*. Paris: Auguste Durand 1862.

Duncan, Hugh Dalziel. *Language and Literature in Society*. Chicago: University of Chicago Press, 1953.

Eastman, Max. *Enjoyment of Laughter*. New York: Simon
    & Schuster, 1936; London: Hamish Hamilton, 1937-

-- *The Sense of Humor*. New York: Scribner's, 1936.

Emerson, Ralph Waldo. "The Comic," *Complete Essays*.
    New York: 1940.

Enck, John J., Elizabeth T. Forter, and Alvin Whitley, eds.
    The Comic in Theory and Practice. New York: Apple-
    ton-Century-Crofts, 1960.

Everett, Charles Carroll. *Poetry, Comedy and Duty*. Bos-
    ton: Houghton Mifflin, 1890.

Farquhar, George. "A Discourse upon Comedy," *Complete
    Works*, vol. 2. London: Nonsuch Press, 1930.

Feibleman, James K. *In Praise of Comedy; A Study in Its
    Theory and Practice*. London: Allen & Unwin; New
    York: Macmillan, 1939; New York: Russell & Russell,
    1962.

-- "The Meaning of Comedy," *Aesthetics*. New York:
    Duell, Sloan & Pearce, 1949. Reprinted in *The Play
    and the Reader*, ed. Stanley Johnson, Judah Bierman
    and James Hart. Englewood Cliffs, N.J.: Prentice-
    Hall, 1966.

Ferenczi, Sandor. "The Psychoanalysis of Wit and the
    Comical," *Further Contributions to the Theory and*

Technique of Psycho-Analysis. London: Hogarth Press, 1926.

Fielding, Henry. "Author's Preface," 1742 *Joseph Andrews*. New York: Reinhart, 1948.

Fitzgerald, Percy H. *Principles of Comedy and Dramatic Effect*. London: 1870.

Foote, Samuel. *The Roman and English Comedy Consider'd and Compar'd. With an Examen into the Merit of the Present Comic Actors*. London: 1747.

Fowler, H. W. "Humour," *A Dictionary of Modern English Usage*. Oxford: Clarendon Press, 1937.

Fox, A. "Humour and Wit," *Cassell's Encyclopaedia of Literature*, vol. I. London: Cassell, 1953.

Freud, Sigmund. *Wit and Its Relation to the Unconscious* 1904, trans. by A. A. Brill. New York: Moffat, Yard, 1917; Random House, 1938. Newly translated from the German as *Jokes and Their Relation to the Unconscious* New York: W. W. Norton; London: Routledge & Kegan Paul, 1960.

Frye, Northrop. "The Argument of Comedy," *English Institute Essays 1948*, ed. D. A. Robertson, Jr. New York: Columbia University Press, 1949.

-- "The Structure of Comedy," *Eight Great Comedies*, ed. Sylvan Barnet, Morton Berman and William Burton. New York: Mentor Books, 1958.

-- "Comic Fictional Modes," *Anatomy of Criticism*. Princeton: Princeton University Press, 1957. Reprinted in *The Play and the Reader*, ed. Stanley Johnson, Judah Bierman and James Hart. Englewood Cliffs: Prentice-Hall, 1966.

Gassner, John. "Comedy and Farce," *Producing the Play*. New York: Holt, Rinehart & Winston, 1953.

-- *Theatre at the Crossroads*. New York: Holt, Rinehart & Winston, 1960.

Gaultier, Paul. *Le rire et la caricature*. Préface par E. Boutroux. Paris: 1906.

Goldsmith, Oliver. "A Comparison between Laughing and Sentimental Comedy [1765]," *The Works of Oliver Goldsmith*, ed. Peter Cunningham. London: John Murray, 1878.

Goodman, Paul. "Comic Plots," *The Structure of Literature*. Chicago: University of Chicago Press, 1954.

Gordon, George. "What Is Comedy?" *Shakespearian Comedy and Other Studies*. Oxford: Clarendon Press, 1944.

Graves, R. *Mrs. Fisher; or, The Future of Humour*. London: Kegan Paul, 1928.

Gregory, J. C. *The Nature of Laughter*. New York: Harcourt, Brace, 1924.

Greig, John Young Thompson. *The Psychology of Laughter and Comedy*. New York: Dodd; London: George Allen & Unwin, 1923.

Grotjahn, Martin. *Beyond Laughter*. New York: McGraw-Hill, 1957.

Hadow, W. H. *The Use of Comic Episodes in Tragedy*. London: English Association, 1907.

Halwyn, B. *An Essay on Comedy* (1782).

Hazlitt, William. "On Wit and Humour [1819]." *Lectures on the English Poets and The English Comic Writers*, ed. William Carew Hazlitt. London: George Bell, 1884.

Herrick, Marvin T. *Comic Theory in the Sixteenth Century*. Urbana, Ill.: University of Illinois Press, 1950.

[Hippisley, John]. *A Dissertation on Comedy, In Which the Rise and Progress of the Species of the Drama Is Particularly Consider'd and Deduc'd from the Earliest to the Present Age*. London: 1750.

Hoy, Cyrus. *The Hyacinth Room; An Investigation into the Nature of Comedy, Tragedy and Tragicomedy*. New York: Knopf; London: Chatto & Windus, 1964.

Hughes, Leo. *A Century of English Farce*. Princeton, N.J.: Princeton University Press, 1956.

Huizinga, Johan. *Home Ludens; A Study of Play-Element in Culture.* Trans. by R. F. C. Hull. London: Routledge & Kegan Paul, 1949.

Hunt, Leigh. *Wit and Humour.* Selected from *The English Poets.* With an Illustrative Essay and Critical Comments. London: Smith, Eder, 1846.

Hutcheson, Francis. *Reflections upon Laughter.* Glasgow: 1750.

Janentzki, Christian. "Über Tragik, Kemik und Humor," *Jahrbuch des Freien Deutschen Hochstifts, 1936—1940* (1940).

Jankélévitch, Vladimir. *L'Ironie.* Paris: Alcan, 1936.

Jekels, Ludwig. "On the Psychology of Comedy," *Selected Papers.* London: Image Publishing Co., 1952.

Jerrold, Walter. "Of Wit and Humour Generally," *A Book of Famous Wits.* London: Methuen, 1912.

Johnson, Samuel. "The Difficulty of Defining Comedy [1751] ," *The Rambler.* London: Dodsley, Owen, 1794.

Kaul, A. N. *The Action of English Comedy; Studies in the Encounter of Abstraction and Experience from Shakespeare to Shaw.* New Haven, Conn.: Yale University

Press, 1970.

Ker, W. P. "On Comedy," *On Modern Literature; Lectures and Addresses*, ed. Terence Spencer and James Sutherland. Oxford: Clarendon Press, 1955.

Kernan, Alvin. *The Cankered Muse*. New Haven, Conn.: Yale University Press, 1959.

-- *The Plot of Satire*. New Haven & London: Yale University Press, 1965.

Kerr, Walter. *Comedy and Tragedy*. London: Bodley Head, 1968.

Kitchin, George. *A Survey of Burlesque and Parody in English*. Edinburgh: Oliver & Boyd, 1931.

Knights, L. C. "Notes on Comedy," *Determinations*, ed. F. R. Leavis. London: Chatto & Windus, 1934. The essay also appeared in *The Importance of Scrutiny*, ed. Eric Bentley. London: George W. Stewart, 1964.

Knox, Norman. *The Word Irony and Its Context, 1500–1755*. Durham: Duke University Press, 1961.

Koestler, Arthur. "The Comic," *Insight and Outlook*. London: Macmillan, 1949.

Kris, Ernest. "Ego Development and the Comic," *Psychoanalytic Explorations in Art*. New York: International Universities Press, 1952. Reprinted from *International Journal of Psycho-Analysis*, (1938).

Kronenberger, Louis. "Some Prefatory Words on Comedy,"
    The Thread of Laughter. New York: Alfred A. Knopf,
    1952. Reprinted in *The Play and the Reader*, ed. Stan-
    ley Johnson, Judah Bierman and James Hart. Englewood
    Cliffs, N.J.: Prentice-Hall, 1966.

Langer, Susanne K. "The Great Dramatic Forms: The Comic
    Rhythm," *Feeling and Form*. New York: Scribner's,
    1953. Reprinted in *Eight Great Comedies*, ed. Sylvan
    Barnet, Morton Berman and William Burto. New York:
    Mentor Books, 1958.

Lauter, Paul, ed. *Theories of Comedy*. Anchor Books. Gar-
    den City, N.Y.: Doubleday, 1964.

Leacock, Stephen. *Humour: Its Theory and Technique*. Lon-
    don: Bodley Head; Toronto: Dodd, Mead, 1935.

-- *Humour and Humanity*. New York: Holt, 1938.

L'Estrange, A. G. K. *History of English Humour and Ancient
    Humour*. New York: Best Books, 1931.

Levy, Gertrude Rachel. "Comedy," *The Gate of Horn*. Lon-
    don: Faber & Faber, 1948.

Lewisohn, Ludwig. "A Note on Comedy," *The Drama and
    the Stage*. New York: Harcourt, Brace, 1922.

Leyburn, Ellen Douglass. "Comedy and Tragedy Transposed"
    The Play and The Reader, ed. Stanley Johnson, Judah

13

Bierman and James Hart. Englewood Cliffs., N.J.: Prentice-Hall, 1966. Reprinted from *Yale Review*, LIII, No. 4 (Summer 1964), 553—562.

Lipps, Theodor. "The Comical and Related Things," *Ästhetik*. Hamburg and Leipzig: L. Voss, 1903.

-- *Komik und Humor*. Hamburg and Leipzig, 1890.

Ludovici, Anthony M. *The Secret of Laughter*. New York: Viking Press, 1933.

Mack, Maynard. "Introduction," *Joseph Andrews*. New York: Reinehart, 1948.

Mathewson, Louise. *Bergson's Theory of the Comic in the Light of English Comedy*. University of Nebraska Studies in Language, Literature, and Criticism No. 5. Lincoln: University of Nebraska Press, 1920.

Menon, V. K. Krishna. *A Theory of Laughter*. London: Georg Allen & Unwin, 1931.

Meredith, George. *An Essay on Comedy and the Uses of the Comic Spirit* [1871], ed. with an Introduction and Notes by Lane Cooper. New York: Scribner's, 1918. With an Introduction and Appendix by Wylie Sypher. Anchor Books Garden City, N.Y.: Doubleday, 1956.

Meyerhold, Vsevolod. "Farce," *Theatre in the Twentieth Century*, ed. Robert W. Corrigan. New York: Grove Press,

1963. Reprinted from *Tulane Drama Review*, IV (September 1959), 139–149.

Mic, Constant. *La Commedia dell'arte*. Paris: Schiffrin, 1927.

Michiels, Alfred. *Le monde du comique et du rire*. Paris, [1886].

Millett, Fred B. and Gerald Eades Bentley. "Comedy," *The Art of the Drama*. New York & London: D. Appleton-Centruy, 1935. •

Monro, D. H. *Argument of Laughter*. Melbourne: University of Melbourne Press, 1951.

Moore, John B. *English Comedy*. New York: Dutton, 1929; London: Dent, 1932.

-- *The Comic and Realistic in English Drama*. Chicago: University of Chicago Press, 1925; Cambridge: Cambridge University Press, 1926; New York: Russell & Russell, 1965.

Morgan, C. Lloyd. "Laughter," *Encyclopedia of Religion and Ethics*, vol. VII. Edinburgh, 1914.

Morris, Corbyn. *An Essay towards Fixing the True Standards of Wit, Humour, Raillery, Satire and Ridicule*. London, 1744; Ann Arbor: Augustan Reprint Society, 1947.

Muir, Kenneth. *The Comedy of Manners*. London: Hutchinson

University Library, 1970.

Nathan, George Jean. "On the Criticism of Laughter," *The World in Falseface*. New York: Alfred A.Knopf, 192⟩

-- "The Test of the Comedian," *The World in Falseface*. New York: Alfred A. Knopf, 1923.

Nicoll, Allardyce. "Comedy," *The Theatre and Dramatic Theory*. London: Harrap, 1962.

Olson, Elder. *The Theory of Comedy*. Bloomington: Indiana University Press, 1970.

Orben, Robert. *Comedy Technique*. Hackensack, N.J.: Wehman Bros., 1951.

Palmer, John. *Comedy*. Art and Craft of Letters Series. London: Martin Secker, [1914]; New York, 1915.

-- *The Comedy of Manners*. London: George Bell, 1913.

Parton, James. *Caricature and Other Comic Art*. New York Harper, 1877.

Perry, Henry Ten Eyck. *Masters of Dramatic Comedy and Their Social Themes*. Cambridge, Mass.: Harvard University Press, 1939; London: Oxford University Press, 1940.

-- "Comedy," *Dictionary of World Literary Terms*. London: Allen & Unwin, 1955.

-- "Theory and Practice of Dramatic Comedy," *The Comic Spirit in Restoration Drama*. London: Oxford University Press, 1925.

Piddington, Ralph. *The Psychology of Laughter; A Study in Social Adaptation*. London: Figurehead, [1933].

Poinsinet de Sivry, Louis. *Traité des causes physiques et morales du rire, relativement à l'art de l'exciter.* Amsterdam, 1768.

Potts, J. L. *Comedy*. London: Hutchinson, 1960.

Quayle, Calvin King. "Humor in Tragedy." Ph.D. Dissertation, University of Minnesota, 1958.

Raulin, J. M. *Le rire et les exhilarants; Etude anatomique, psychophysiologique et pathologique.* Paris, 1900.

Reisner, C. F. "Comedy," *A Hundred Movie-Goers Must Be Right*, by I. Price. Cleveland: Movie Appreciation Press, 1939.

Repplier, Agnes. *In Pursuit of Laughter*. Boston: Houghto
Mifflin, 1936.

Roberts, Michael. "Wit and Humour," *Chambers's Encyclo
paedia*, vol. XIV (1959), pp. 624—625.

Rogers, Will. *Wit and Wisdom*. New York: Stokes, 1936.

Rowe, Kenneth Thorpe. "Functions and Values," *Write T
Play*. New York & London: Funk & Wagnalls, 1939.

Santayana, George. "The Comic Mask," *Soliloquies in En
land*. London: Constable, 1922.

Sawyer, Newell W. *The Comedy of Manners from Sheridan
to Maugham*. Philadelphia: University of Pennsylvania
Press, 1931.

Schiller, Friedrich. "On Simple and Sentimental Poetry,"
[1795] *Essays Aesthetical and Philosophical*. London:
George Bell, 1884.

Schilling, Bernard N. *The Comic Spirit: Boccaccio to
Thomas Mann*. Detroit: Wayne State University Press,
1965.

Seward, Samuel S. *The Paradox of the Ludicrous*. [Palo
Alto]: Stanford University Press, 1930.

Seyler, Athene and Stephen Haggard. *The Craft of Comedy*
London: J. Garnet Miller, 1958.

Shaw, Bernard. ''Meredith on Comedy,'' *Our Theatres in the Nineties*. London: Constable, 1932.

Sidis, Boris. *The Psychology of Laughter*. New York & London: D. Appleton, 1913.

Simpson, Harold. *Excursions in Comedy*. London: Besant, 1930.

   -- *Excursions in Farce*. London: Besant, 1930.

Skinner, B. F. *Verbal Behavior*. New York: Appleton-Century-Crofts, 1957.

Smith, Willard M. *The Nature of Comedy*. Boston: Gorham Press, 1931.

Stevenson, David Lloyd. *The Love-Game Comedy*. Columbia University Studies in English and Comparative Literature, No. 164. New York: Columbia University Press, 1946.

Steward, Samuel S., Jr. *The Paradox of the Ludicrous*. Stanford, Calif.: Stanford University Press, 1930.

Stoll, E. E. ''The Comic Method,'' *Shakespeare Studies; Historical and Comparative in Method*. New York: Frederick Ungar, 1960.

Sully, James. *An Essay on Laughter, Its Forms, Its Causes, Its Development and Its Value*. London & New York: Longmans, 1902.

Swabey, Marie Collins. *Comic Laughter; A Philosophical*

Essay. New Haven: Yale University Press, 1961.

Sypher, Wylie. "The Meanings of Comedy." Appended to *Comedy*, by Bergson and Meredith. Anchor Books. Garden City, N.Y.: Doubleday, 1956.

Taylor, W. D., ed. *Eighteenth-Century Comedy*. Oxford: Oxford University Press, 1929.

Thompson, Alan Reynolds. "Comedy," *The Anatomy of Drama*. Berkeley & Los Angeles: University of California Press, 1942.

-- *The Dry Mock; A Study of Irony in Drama*. Berkeley & Los Angeles: University of California Press, 1948.

Thomson, J. A. K. *Irony; An Historical Introduction*. London: G. Allen & Unwin, 1926.

Thorndike, Ashley H. *English Comedy*. New York: Macmillan, 1929.

Vasey, George. *The Philosophy of Laughter and Smiling*. London, 1875.

Villiers, Andre. *La psychologie du comedien*. Paris, 1942

Walpole, Horace. "Thoughts on Comedy," *Works,* vol. II London, 1798.

Wells, Carolyn. *An Outline of Humour.* New York: Putnam, 1923.

Welsford, Enid. *The Fool: His Social and Literary History.* London: Faber & Faber, 1935.

Whipple, E. P. "Wit and Humour," *Lectures on Subjects Connected with Literature and Life.* Boston, Mass., 1850.

White, E. B. "Some Remarks on Humor," *The Second Tree from the Corner.* New York: Harper, 1954.

Willeford, William. *The Fool and His Scepter; A Study in Clowns and Their Audience.* Evanston: Northwestern University Press; London: Edward Arnold, 1969.

Wimsatt, W. K., Jr., ed. *English Stage Comedy.* English Institute Essays, 1954. London: Oxford University Press, 1956.

-- *The Idea of Comedy; Essays in Prose and Verse: Ben Jonson to George Meredith.* Englewood Cliffs, N.J.: Prentice-Hall, 1969.

Worcester, David. *The Art of Satire.* Cambridge, Mass.: Harvard University Press, 1940.

Wright, Thomas. *A History of Caricature and Grotesque in Literature and Art.* London: Virtue, 1865.

(b) Periodicals

Auden, W. H. "Notes on the Comic," *Thought*, XXVII (Spri▮ 1952), 57–71.

Bawdon, H. Heath. "The Comic As Illustrating the Summation – Irradiation Theory of Pleasure – Pain," *Psychological Review* (Baltimore), XVII, No. 5 (September 1910), 336–346.

Behrman, S. N. "What Makes Comedy High?" *New York Tim* (30 March 1952), Section 2, p. 1. Reprinted in *American Playwrights on Drama*, ed. Horst Frenz. New York: Hill & Wang, 1965.

Bliss, Silvia H. "The Origin of Laughter," *American Journal of Psychology* (Albany, N.Y.), XXVI, No. 2 (April 1915), 236–246.

Brill, A. A. "Freud's Theory of Wit," *Journal of Abnormal and Social Psychology*, VI (October-November 1911).

Brody, Morris W. "The Meaning of Laughter," *Psychoanaly Quarterly* (N.Y.), (1950).

Brown, Ivor. "Some Facts about Fun," *Illustrated London News*, CXCII (12 May 1938), 915.

-- "British Comedy," *Theatre Arts Monthly* (N.Y.), XIX

(August 1935), 585—593.

Carritt, E. F. "A Theory of the Ludicrous," *The Hibbert Journal* (London), XXI, No. 3 (April 1923), 552—564.

Carus, Paul. "On the Philosophy of Laughing," *Monist* (Chicago), VIII, No. 2 (January 1898), 250—272.

Chapman, John Jay. "The Comic," *Hibbert Journal* (London), VIII, No. 4 (July 1910), 862—872.

Courtney, W. L. "The Idea of Comedy," *Fortnightly Review* (London & N.Y.), XCV, New Series (May 1914), 843—858. Reprinted in *Old Saws and Modern Instances* (London: Chapman & Hall, 1918), pp. 122—160.

Duerrenmatt, Friedrich. "Problems of the Theatre," *Tulane Drama Review* (1958).

Dugas, L. "La fonction psychologique du rire," *Revue philosophique*, LXII (1906).

Eberhart, Richard. "Tragedy as Limitation: Comedy as Control and Resolution," *Tulane Drama Review*, VI, No. 4 (June 1962), 3—14.

Fadiman, C. "Six Comedies in Search of Something,"
  Stage, XII (May 1935), 18–19.

Fleming, Rudd. "Of Contrast Between Tragedy and Comedy,"
  Journal of Philosophy (N.Y.), XXXVI, No. 20 (28 September 1939), 543–553.

Fry, Christopher. "Comedy," *The Adelphi* (London), XXVI
  No. 1 (November 1950), 27–29.

  -- "Comedy," *Tulane Drama Review*, IV (March 1960), 70–
  79.

Gilder, Rosamond. "Merriment Through the Ages," *Theatre
  Arts Monthly* (N.Y.), XIX (October 1935), 770–779.

  -- , et al. "In the Service of Comedy," *Theatre Arts Month*
  (N.Y.), XX (September 1938), 635–694.

Gilman, Bradley. "The Ethical Element in Wit and Humor,"
  International Journal of Ethics (Philadelphia), XIX (July
  1909), 488–494.

Guthrie, William Norman. "The Theory of the Comic," *The
  International Quarterly* (June-September 1903), 254–264.

Hall, G. Stanley. "The Psychology of Tickling, Laughing,
  and the Comic," *American Journal of Psychology* (Worcester, Mass.), IX, No. 1 (October 1897), 1–41.

Hamilton, Edith. "Comedy," *Theatre Arts Monthly* (N.Y.), XI (July 1927), 503–512.

Hollingworth, H. L. "Experimental Studies in Judgment: Judgments of the Comic," *Psychological Review* (N.Y.), XVIII, No. 2 (March 1911), 132–156.

Hoy, Cyrus. "Comedy, Tragedy, and Tragicomedy," *Virginia Quarterly Review* (Charlottesville), XXXVI, No. 1 (Winter 1960), 105–118.

Hurrell, John Dennis. "A Note on Farce," *Quarterly Journal of Speech*, XLV (December 1959), 426–430.

Hutton, James. "The Value of Beauty and Wonder in Comedy," *Classical Weekly*, XVIII (15 December 1924), 68–70.

Kallen, Horace M. "The Aesthetic Principle in Comedy," *American Journal of Psychology* (Worcester, Mass.), XXII, No. 2 (April 1911), 137–157.

Kantor, J. R. "An Attempt Toward a Naturalistic Description of Emotions," *Psychological Review* (N.Y.), XXVIII, No. 1 (January 1921), 19–42; XXVIII, No. 2 (March 1921), 120–140.

Kimmins, C. W. "Visual Humour," *The Strand Magazine* (London) (April 1922), 294–299.

Kline, L. W. "The Psychology of Humour," *American Journal of Psychology* (Worcester, Mass.), XVIII (October 1907), 421–441.

Kris, Ernest. "Ego Development and the Comic," *International Journal of Psycho-Analysis* (1938). Reprinted in *Psychoanalytic Explorations in Art* (New York: International Universities Press, 1952).

Krutch, Joseph Wood. "The Fundamentals of Farce," *Theatre Arts Monthly* (N.Y.), XL, No. 7 (July 1956), 29–30, 92–93.

Lesser, S. "Tragedy, Comedy, and the Esthetic Experience *Literature and Psychology*, VI (1956), 131–139.

Leveque, Charles. "Le rire, le comique, et le risible, dans l'esprit et dans l'art," *Revue des deux mondes*, 2me periode, tome 47 (September 1863), 107–139.

Lewis, Wyndham. "Studies in the Art of Laughter," *London Mercury*, XXX, No. 180 (October 1934), 509–515.

Leyburn, Ellen Douglass. "Comedy and Tragedy Transpose *The Yale Review*, LIII, No. 4 (Summer 1964), 553–562. Reprinted in *The Play and the Reader*, ed. Stanley Johns Judah Bierman, and James Hart (Englewood Cliffs, N.J.: Prentice-Hall, 1966).

Lilly, W. S. "Theory of the Ludicrous," *Fortnightly Review* (London), LIX (May 1896), 724–737.

Lou, Kwang Lai. "Theories of Laughter," *The Chinese Students Monthly*, XVII, No. 2 (December 1921), 102–113.

MacCarthy, Desmond. "Artificial Comedy," *New Statesman and Nation* (London), XVIII (26 August 1939), 305–307.

Mack, Maynard. "The Muse of Satire," *Yale Review*, XLI, No. 1 (Autumn 1951), 80–92.

Macnaughtan, S. "Humour," *Nineteenth Century and After* (London), CCCCXL (October 1913), 803–813.

Martin, Lillien J. "Psychology of Aesthetics: Experimental Prospecting in the Field of the Comic," *American Journal of Psychology*, XVI (1905).

Melinand, Camille. "Pourquoi rit-on? Etude sur la cause psychologique du rire," *Revue des deux mondes*, CXXVII (February 1895), 612–630.

Meyerhold, Vsevolod. "Farce," translated by Nora Beeson, *Tulane Drama Review*, IV (September 1959), 139–149. Reprinted in *Theatre in the Twentieth Century*, ed. Robert W. Corrigan (New York: Grove Press, 1963).

Morrison, Jack. "A Note Concerning Investigations on the Constancy of Audience Laughter," *Sociometry; A Journal of Inter-Personal Relations* (N.Y.), III, No. 2 (April 1940), 179–185.

Muggeridge, Malcolm. "My First Acquaintance with Humour," *English* (London), IX, No. 55 (Spring 1954), 2–4.

Palmer, John. "Comedy and Cant," *Saturday Review* (London),

CXVII (1914), 334.

-- "Comedy Again and Cant," *Saturday Review* (London), CXVII (1914), 366.

Penjon, A. "Le rire et la liberte," *Revue philosophique*, (1893).

Read, Herbert. "The Definition of Comedy," *Dial* (Chicago) LXXVI (March 1924), 257–264.

Reynolds, George F. "Comedy and the Crisis," *Western Humanities Review* (Utah), V (Spring 1951), 143–151.

Spencer, Herbert. "The Physiology of Laughter," *Macmillan's Magazine* (Cambridge), I (March 1860), 395–402 .

Spivack, Charlotte K. "Tragedy and Comedy: A Metaphysical Wedding," *Bucknell Review*, IX (1960), 212–223.

Stephenson, Robert C. "Farce As Method," *Tulane Drama Review*, V, No. 2 (December 1960), 85–93.

Stolnitz, Jerome. "Notes on Comedy and Tragedy," *Philosophy and Phenomenological Research* (Buffalo, N.Y.), XVI, No. 1 (September 1955), 45–60.

Thurber, James. "The Future, If Any, of Comedy," *Times Literary Supplement* (11 August 1961), 512–513.

-- "The Case for Comedy," *The Atlantic* (Boston), CCVI, No. 5 (November 1960), 97–99.

Vexler, Julius. "The Essence of Comedy," *Sewanee Review*, XLIII (July-September 1935), 292–310.

Watts, Harold H. "The Sense of Regain: A Theory of Comedy," *The University of Kansas City Review* (1940).

Young, Stark. "Concerning Comedy," *New Republic*, LIX (19 June 1929), 127–128.

A BIBLIOGRAPHY OF CRITICAL STUDIES

Tragedy

(a) Books

Anderson, Maxwell. *The Essence of Tragedy*. Washington: Anderson House, 1939.

Aristotle. *Poetics*.

Aylen, Leo. *Greek Tragedy and the Modern World*. London: Methuen, 1964.

Bahnsen, Julius. *Das Tragische und der Humor*. Leipzig: J. A. Barth, 1931.

Barret, B. "The Causes of the Pleasure Which Is Derived from Tragedy," *Pretention to a Final Analysis of the Nature of Sublimity* (1812).

Barrett, William. *Irrational Man; A Study in Existential Philosophy*. Garden City, N.Y.: Doubleday, 1958.

Benson, Carl and Taylor Littleton. *The Idea of Tragedy*. Glenview, Ill.: Scott, Foresman, 1966.

Bentley, Eric. *The Modern Theatre*. London: Robert Hale, 1948.

Berdyaev, Nicolas. *The Destiny of Man*. Translated by Natalie Duddington. London: Geoffrey Bles, 1937.

Bodkin, Maud. *Archetypal Patterns in Poetry; Psychological Studies of Imagination*. London: Oxford University Press, 1934.

Bogard, Travis and William I. Oliver, eds. *Modern Drama; Essays in Criticism*. New York: Oxford University Press, 1965.

Bradley, A. C. "Hegel's Theory of Tragedy," *Oxford Lectures on Poetry*. London: Macmillan, 1909.

-- *Shakespearean Tragedy*. London: Macmillan, 1905.

Bredvold, Louis I. "The Modern Temper and Tragic Drama, *The Play and the Reader*, ed. Stanley Johnson, Judiah Bierman and James Hart. Englewood Cliffs, N.J.: Prentice-Hall, 1966. Reprinted from *Michigan Alumnus Quarterly*, LXI, No. 18 (21 May 1955).

Brooks, Cleanth, ed. *Tragic Themes in Western Literature*. New Haven & London: Yale University Press, 1955.

-- and Robert B. Heilman. *Understanding Drama*. New York: Henry Holt, 1961.

Brunetiere, Ferdinand. "L.'evolution d'un genre: la tragedie, *Etudes critiques sur l'histoire de la litterature francaise*, seventh series, 2 nd ed. (Paris, 1905).

Burke, Kenneth. "Dialectic of Tragedy," *A Grammar of Motives*. New York: Prentice-Hall, 1945.

Campbell, Joseph. "Tragedy and Comedy," *The Hero with a Thousand Faces*. Bollingen Series, XVII. New York: Pantheon Books, 1949.

Campbell, Lewis. *Tragic Drama in Aeschylus, Sophocles, and Shakespeare*. London: Smith, Elder, 1904.

Cook, Albert. *The Dark Voyage and the Golden Mean*. Cambridge, Mass.: Harvard University Press, 1949.

Corrigan, Robert W., ed. *Tragedy: Vision and Form*. San Francisco: Chandler, 1965.

Courtney, W. L. *The Idea of Tragedy in Ancient and Modern Drama*. Westminster: Archibald Constable, 1900.

De Unamuno, Miguel. *The Tragic Sense of Life*. London: Macmillan, 1931.

De Witt, Norman J. "Tragedy and Personal Humanism." Prefixed to *Renunciation as a Tragic Focus*, by E. H. Falk. Minneapolis: University of Minnesota Press, 1954.

Dixon, W. Macneile. *Tragedy*. London: Edward Arnold, 1924.

Dodds, E. R. *The Greeks and the Irrational*. Sather Classical Lectures, vol. 25. Berkeley & Los Angeles: University of California Press, 1951.

Drew, Elizabeth. "Tragedy," *Discovering Drama*. New York: W. W. Norton; London: Jonathan Cape, 1937.

Else, G. F. *Aristotle's Poetics: The Argument*. Cambridge Mass.: Harvard University Press, 1957.

Falk, Eugene H. *Renunciation as a Tragic Focus*. Minneapolis: University of Minnesota Press, 1954.

Fergusson, Francis. "The Tragic Rhythm of Action," *The Idea of a Theatre*. Princeton, N.J.: Princeton University Press, 1949.

-- *The Human Image in Dramatic Literature*. Garden City, N.Y.: Doubleday, 1957.

[Francklin, T.] *A Dissertation on Ancient Tragedy*. London, 1760.

Frye, Northrop. *Anatomy of Criticism; Four Essays*. Princeton, N.J.: Princeton University Press; London: Oxford University Press, 1957.

Frye, Prosser H. *Romance and Tragedy*. Boston, 1922; Lincoln: University of Nebraska Press, 1961.

Gassner, John. "The Possibilities and Perils of Modern Tragedy," *Theatre and Drama in the Making*, ed. John Gassner and Ralph G. Allen. Boston: Houghton Mifflin, 1964. Reprinted from *Tulane Drama Review*, I (June 1957), 3—14.

-- "Tragedy," *Producing the Play*. New York: Holt, Rinehart & Winston, 1953.

-- *The Theatre in Our Times*. New York: Crown Publishers, 1954.

-- *Theatre at Crossroads*. New York: Holt, Rinehart & Winston, 1960.

Geddes, Virgil. *Beyond Tragedy*. Seattle: University of Washington Book Store, 1930.

Glicksberg, Charles I. *The Tragic Vision in 20th Century Literature*. New York: Dell, 1963.

Goodman, Paul. "Serious Plots," *The Structure of Literature*. Chicago: University of Chicago Press, 1954.

Greene, W. C. "The Idea of Tragedy," *Moira; Fate, Good and Evil in Greek Thought*. Cambridge, Mass.: Harvard University Press; London: Oxford University Press, 1944.

Guthke, Karl S. *Modern Tragicomedy; An Investigation into the Nature of the Genre*. New York: Random House, 1966.

Guthrie, William. *An Essay upon English Tragedy. With Remarks upon the Abbe de Blanc's Observations on the English Stage*. London: T. Waller, 1757.

Hadow, W. H. *The Use of Comic Episodes in Tragedy*. London: English Association, 1907.

Hale, Edward Everett, Jr. "Our Idea of Tragedy," *Dramatists of Today*. New York: Henry Holt, 1911.

Hallman, Ralph J. *Psychology of Literature*. New York: Philosophical Library, 1961.

Harris, Mark. *The Case for Tragedy*. New York: G. P. Putnam's, 1932.

Hathorn, Richmond Y. *Tragedy, Myth and Mystery*. Bloomington, Ind.: Indiana University Press, 1963.

Henn, T. R. *The Harvest of Tragedy*. London: Methuen, 1956; University Paperbacks, 1966.

Herrick, Marvin T. *Tragicomedy: Its Origin and Developmer in Italy, France and England*. Illinois Studies in Langua and Literature, XXXIX. Urbana: University of Illinois Press, 1955; repr., 1962.

Hodson, William. "Observations on Tragedy," *Zoraida*. Lo don: G. Kearsly, 1780.

Hoy, Cyrus. *The Hyacinth Room; An Investigation into the Nature of Comedy, Tragedy and Tragicomedy*. New Yorl Knopf; London: Chatto & Windus, 1964.

Hume, David. "Of Tragedy," *Essays and Treatises on Sev eral Subjects*, vol. I. Edinburgh: Bell & Bradfute, 1825.

Huxley, Aldous. "Tragedy and the Whole Truth," *Music at Night and Other Essays*. New York: Fountain Press, 19 London: Chatto & Windus, 1949; Harmondsworth: Pengu Books, 1950.

38

Jacquot, Jean. *Le theatre tragique*. Paris: Editions du centre national de la recherche scientifique, 1962.

Janentzki, Christian. "Uber Tragik, Komik und Humor," *Jahrbuch des Freien Deutschen Hochstifts, 1936–1940* (1940).

Jaspers, Karl. *Tragedy Is Not Enough*. Trans. by Harald A. T. Reiche, Harry T. Moore and Karl W. Deutsch. Boston: The Beacon Press, 1952; London: Victor Gollan cz, 1953.

Jeffers, Robinson. "The Tower Beyond Tragedy," *American Playwrights on Drama*, ed. Horst Frenz. New York: Hill & Wang, 1965.

Jekels, Ludwig. "The Psychology of Pity," *Selected Papers*. London: Image Publishing Co., 1952.

Jepsen, Laura. *Ethical Aspects of Tragedy*. Gainesville: University of Florida Press, 1953.

Joseph, B. L. *The Tragic Actor; Survey of Tragic Acting in England from Burbage to Irving*. London: Routledge & Kegan Paul, 1959.

Kerr, Walter. *Comedy and Tragedy*. London: Bodley Head, 1968.

Kierkegaard, Soren. *Fear and Trembling*. Translated from the Danish by Robert Payne. London & New York:

Oxford University Press, 1939.

Kitto, H. D. F. *Form and Meaning in Drama*. London: Methuen, 1956; New York: Barnes & Noble, 1960; University Paperbacks, 1960.

Koestler, Arthur. *The Age of Longing*. New York, 1951.

Krieger, Murray. *The Tragic Vision; Variations on a Theme in Literary Interpretation*. New York: Holt, Rinehart & Winston, 1960.

Krook, Dorothea. *Elements of Tragedy*. New Haven & London: Yale University Press, 1969.

Krutch, Joseph Wood. "The Tragic Fallacy," *The Modern Temper; A Study and a Confession*. New York: Harcourt Brace, 1929; London: Jonathan Cape, 1930. Reprinted from *Atlantic Monthly* (Boston), CXLII (November 1928), 601–611.

-- *'Modernism' in Modern Drama; A Definition and an Estimate*. Ithaca, N.Y.: Cornell University Press, 1953.

Langer, Susanne K. "The Great Dramatic Forms: The Tragi Rhythm," *Feeling and Form*. London: Routledge & Kegan Paul; New York: Scribner's, 1953.

Leavis, F. R. "Tragedy and the 'Medium'," *The Common Pursuit*. London: Chatto & Windus, 1952.

Leech, Clifford. *Tragedy*. The Critical Idiom Series. London: Methuen, 1969.

Lerner, Max. "A Fatal Family," *The Play and the Reader,* ed. Stanley Johnson, Judah Bierman and James Hart. Englewood Cliffs, N.J.: Prentice-Hall, 1966.

Levy, Gertrude Rachel. "Tragedy," *The Gate of Horn.* London: Faber & Faber, 1948.

Lewisohn, Ludwig. "A Note on Tragedy," *The Drama and the Stage.* New York: Harcourt, Brace, 1922.

Lucas, F. L. *Tragedy in Relation to Aristotle's Poetics.* London: Hogarth Press, 1927; New York: Harcourt, Brace, 1928.

MacCollom, William G. *Tragedy*. New York: Macmillan, 1957.

McDermot, M. *A Philosophical Inquiry into the Source of the Pleasures Derived from Tragic Representations.* London: Sherwood, Jones, 1824.

Mandel, Oscar. *A Definition of Tragedy.* New York: New York University Press, 1961.

Margeson, J. M. R. *The Origins of English Tragedy.* Oxford: Clarendon Press, 1967.

Mendell, Clarence W. *Our Seneca.* New Haven: Yale University Press; London: Oxford University Press, 1941.

Michel, Laurence. *The Thing Contained; Theory of the Tragic.* Bloomington: Indiana University Press, 1970.

-- and Richard B. Sewall, eds. *Tragedy: Modern Essays in Criticism.* Englewood Cliffs, N.J.: Prentice-Hall, 1963.

Miller, Arthur. "Introduction," *Collected Plays.* New York 1957; London: Cresset, 1958.

-- "Tragedy and the Common Man," *The Play and the Rea* er, ed. Stanley Johnson, Judah Bierman, and James Har' Englewood Cliffs, N.J.: Prentice-Hall, 1966. Also in *American Playwrights on Drama,* ed. Horst Frenz. New York: Hill & Wang, 1965. Reprinted from *Theatre Arts* (N.Y.), XXXV, No. 3 (March 1951), 48–50.

Millett, Fred B. and Gerald Eades Bentley. "Tragedy," *The Art of the Drama.* New York & London: D. Appleton Century, 1935.

Moor, James. *On the End of Tragedy According to Aristotle* Glasgow, 1763.

Morrell, Roy. "The Psychology of Tragic Pleasure," *The Play and the Reader,* ed. Stanley Johnson, Judah Bierma and James Hart. Englewood Cliffs, N.J.: Prentice-Hall, 1966. Reprinted from *Essays in Criticism* (Oxford), VI, No. 1 (January 1956), 22–37.

Muller, Herbert J. *The Spirit of Tragedy.* New York: Alfred

A. Knopf, 1956.

Myers, Henry A. *Tragedy: A View of Life*. Ithaca, N.Y.: Cornell University Press, 1956.

Niebuhr, Reinhold. *Beyond Tragedy*. London: Nisbet, 1938.

Nietzsche, Friedrich. *The Birth of Tragedy*. Trans. by William A. Haussmann. Ed. Oscar Levy. In *Works*, vol. I. Edinburgh & London: T. Fisher Unwin, 1909.

O'Connor, William Van. *Climates of Tragedy*. Baton Rouge, La., 1943; New York: Russell & Russell, 1965.

Olson, Elder. *Tragedy and the Theory of Drama*. Detroit: Wayne State University Press, 1961.

Peckham, Morse. *Beyond the Tragic Vision*. New York: George Braziller, 1962.

Pickard-Cambridge, A. W. *Dithyramb, Tragedy and Comedy*. Oxford: Clarendon Press, 1927.

[Pickering, Roger]. *Reflections upon Theatrical Expression in Tragedy*. London, 1755.

Prior, Moody E. *The Language of Tragedy*. New York:

Comedy and Tragedy

Columbia University Press, 1947.

Quayle, Calvin King. "Humor in Tragedy." Ph.D. Dissertation, University of Minnesota, 1958.

Raglan, Lord. *The Hero; A Study in Tradition, Myth, and Drama*. London: Methuen, 1936; New York, 1937.

Rahill, Frank. *The World of Melodrama*. University Park & London: Pennsylvania State University Press, 1967.

Rank, Otto. *Myth and the Birth of the Hero*. New York, 195

Ransom, J. C. "The Cathartic Principle" and "The Mimem Principle," *The World's Body*. New York & London: C. Scribner's Sons, 1938.

Raphael, D. D. *The Paradox of Tragedy*. The Mahlon Powe Lectures, 1959. Bloomington: Indiana University Press, 1959; London: George Allen & Unwin, 1960.

Rapin, Rene. *Reflections on Aristotle's Treatise of Poesie* London: H. Herringman, 1694.

Richards, I. A. *Principles of Literary Criticism*. London: Kegan Paul; New York: Harcourt, Brace, 1925, pp. 245 f

[Richardson, William] . *Cursory Remarks on Tragedy, on Shakespeare, and on Certain Italian and French Poets,*

Principally Tragedians. London, 1774.

Ridgeway, William. *The Origin of Tragedy*. Cambridge: Cambridge University Press, 1910.

Ristine, Frank Humphrey. *English Tragicomedy: Its Origin and History*. New York: Columbia University Press, 1910.

Robertson, J. G. *Lessing's Dramatic Theory*. Cambridge: Cambridge University Press, 1939.

Rosenmeyer, Thomas G. *The Masks of Tragedy*. Austin: University of Texas Press, 1963.

Rowe, Kenneth Thorpe. "Functions and Values," *Write That Play*. New York & London: Funk & Wagnalls, 1939.

Rymer, Thomas. *A Short View of Tragedy*, 2 parts. London, 1692–1693; Menston: Scholar Press, 1970.

Schlegel, A. W. *A Course of Lectures on Dramatic Art and Literature*, trans. by John Black, 2 vols. London, 1815.

Schopenhauer, Arthur. *The World as Will and Idea*, trans. by R. B. Haldane and J. Kemp, 3 vols. English and Foreign Philosophical Library vols. 22–24. London: Trubner, 1883–1886.

Scott, Nathan A., Jr., ed. *The Tragic Vision and the Christian Faith*. New York: Association Press, 1957.

Sebeok, A., ed. *Myth: A Symposium.* Philadelphia, 1955.

Sewall, Richard B. *The Vision of Tragedy.* New Haven: Yale University Press, 1959.

Shattuck, Charles H. *Tragedy.* Riverside Studies in Literature. Boston: Houghton-Mifflin,

Snell, Bruno. *The Discovery of the Mind,* trans. by T. G. Rosenmyer. Cambridge, Mass.: Harvard University Press Oxford: Basil Blackwell, 1953.

Steiner, George. *The Death of Tragedy.* London: Faber & Faber, 1961.

Styan, J. L. *The Dark Comedy; The Development of Modern Comic Tragedy.* Cambridge: Cambridge University Press 1962.

Thompson, Alan Reynolds. *The Anatomy of Drama.* Berkeley & Los Angeles: University of California Press, 1946, chap. VIII "Melodrama and Tragedy"; and chap. VIII "The Dilemma of Modern Tragedy".

Thorndike, Ashley H. *Tragedy.* Types of English Literature Series. Boston: Houghton-Mifflin, 1908.

Trapp, Joseph. "An Essay upon the Nature and Art of Moving the Passions in Tragedy," *The Works of Virgil.* (1731).

Unamuno, Miguel de. *The Tragic Sense of Life*, trans. by
J. E. C. Flitch. London: Macmillan, 1921.

Vaughan, C. E. *Types of Tragic Drama*. London: Macmillan,
1924.

Volkelt, Johannes. *Asthetic des Tragischen*. Muchen: Beck,
1906.

Weisinger, Herbert. *Tragedy and the Paradox of the Fortunate
Fall*. East Lansing: Michigan State College Press; London: Routledge & Kegan Paul, 1953.

Wertham, Frederick. *Dark Legend; A Study in Murder*. New
York: Duell, Sloan & Pearce, 1941.

Wheelwright, Philip. *The Burning Fountain; A Study in the
Language of Symbolism*. Bloomington: Indiana University Press, 1954.

Whitmore, Charles Edward. *The Supernatural in Tragedy*.
Cambridge, Mass.: Harvard University Press, 1915.

Williams, Raymond. *Modern Tragedy*. Stanford: Stanford
University Press, 1966.

Yeats, W. B. "The Tragic Theatre," *The Cutting of an Agate*.
New York: Macmillan, 1912.

(b) Periodicals

Adolf, Helen. "The Essence and Origin of Tragedy," *Journal of Aesthetics and Art Criticism*, X, No. 2 (December 1951), 112–125.

Arestad, S. "Ibsen's Concept of Tragedy," *PMLA*, LXXIV (1959), 285–297.

Bell, C. G. "Tragedy," *Diogenes* (London), No. 7 (1954), 12–32.

Bredvold, Louis I. "The Modern Temper and Tragic Drama, *Michigan Alumnus Quarterly*, LXI, No. 18 (21 May 1955). Reprinted in *The Play and the Reader*, ed. Stanley Johnson, Judiah Bierman, and James Hart. Englewood Cliffs N.J.: Prentice-Hall, 1966.

Brereton, Geoffrey. "The Hidden God: Some Comments on the Problem of Tragedy." B.B.C. Third Programme, 29 January 1951.

Clay, J. H. "A New Theory of Tragedy: A Description and Evaluation," *Educational Theatre Journal* (Ann Arbor, Mich.), VIII (1956), 295–305.

Coffman, George R. "Tragedy and a Sense of the Tragic in

Some of Its Ethical Implications," *Sewanee Review*, L (January-March 1942), 26—34.

Crocker, L. G. "Mr. Bell on Tragedy," *Diogenes* (London), No. 15 (1956), 112—120.

Doering, J. "David Hume and the Theory of Tragedy," *Modern Language Notes* (Baltimore), LII (December 1937), 1130—1134.

Drucker, Peter F. "The Unfashionable Kierkegaard," *Sewanee Review*, LVII, No. 4 (Autumn 1949), 587—602.

Eberhart, Richard. "Tragedy as Limitation; Comedy as Control and Resolution," *Tulane Drama Review*, VI, No. 4 (June 1962), 3—14.

Fauconnier, R. L. "Tragedy and the Modern Theatre," *Queen's Quarterly* (Kingston, Ont.), LV (1948), 327—332 .

Fiedler, Leslie. "Our Country and Our Culture," *Partisan Review* (N.Y.), XIX, No. 3 (May-June 1952), 294—298.

Frye, Northrop. "The Archetypes of Literature," *Kenyon Review*, XIII, No. 1 (Winter 1951), 92—110.

Gassner, John. "The Possibilities and Perils of Modern Tragedy," *Tulane Drama Review*, I (June 1957), 3–14. Reprinted in *Theatre and Drama in the Making*, ed. John Gassner and Ralph G. Allen (Boston: Houghton Mifflin, 1964).

Griffith, Hubert. "Tragedy and the Box Office," *New Statesman and Nation* (London), III, No. 69, New Series (18 June 1932), 795–797.

Heilman, Robert B. "Tragedy and Melodrama; Speculations on Generic Form," *Texas Quarterly*, III, No. 2 (Summer 1960), 36–50.

Hoy, Cyrus. "Comedy, Tragedy, and Tragicomedy," *Virginia Quarterly Review* (Charlottesville), XXVI, No. 1 (Winter 1960), 105–118.

Jarrett, James L. "Tragedy; A Study in Explication," *ETC: A Review of General Semantics*, XII, No. 3 (Spring 1955), 189–197.

Kimmelman, George. "The Concept of Tragedy in Modern Criticism," *Journal of Aesthetics and Art Criticism*, IV, No. 3 (March 1946), 141–160.

Krieger, Murray. "Tragedy and the Tragic Vision," *Kenyon*

Review, XX, No. 2 (Spring 1958), 281–299.

Krutch, Joseph Wood. "The Tragic Fallacy," *Atlantic Monthly* (Boston), CXLII (November 1928), 601–611. Reprinted in *The Modern Temper; A Study and a Confession* (New York: Harcourt, Brace, 1929; London: Jonathan Cape, 1930).

Lesser, S. "Tragedy, Comedy, and the Esthetic Experience," *Literature and Psychology*, VI (1956), 131–139.

Leyburn, Ellen Douglass. "Comedy and Tragedy Transposed," *Yale Review*, LIII, No. 4 (Summer 1964), 553–562.

Michel, Laurence. "The Possibility of a Christian Tragedy," *Thought* (N.Y.) (1956).

Miller, Arthur. "Tragedy and the Common Man," *Theatre Arts* (N.Y.), XXXV, No. 3 (March 1951), 48–50. Reprinted from *New York Times* (27 February 1949), Section 2, p. 1. Reprinted in *The Play and the Reader*, ed. Stanley Johnson, Judah Bierman and James Hart (Englewood Cliffs, N.J.: Prentice-Hall, 1966); and in *American Playwrights on Drama*, ed. Horst Frenz (New York: Hill & Wang, 1965).

Montague, C. E. "Delights of Tragedy," *The London Mercury*, XIX, No. 110 (December 1928), 133–142.

Moravia, Alberto. "The Sterility of Suffering," *Yale Review*, XLVII, No. 2 (Winter 1958), 175—181.

Morrell, Roy. "The Psychology of Tragic Pleasure," *Essays in Criticism* (Oxford), VI, No. 1 (January 1956), 22—37. Reprinted in *The Play and the Reader*, ed. Stanley Johnson, Judah Bierman and James Hart (Englewood Cliffs, N.J.: Prentice-Hall, 1966).

Murray, A. Victor. "The Divine Tragedy," *The Hibbert Journal* (London), LII (October 1954), 19—24.

Philipson, M. H. "Some Reflections on Tragedy," *Journal of Philosophy* (N.Y.), LV (1958), 197—203.

Pottle, Frederick A. "Catharsis," *Yale Review*, XL, No. 4 (Summer 1951), 621—641.

Quinn, Arthur Hobson. "In Defence of Melodrama," *Bookman* (N.Y.), LXI, No. 4 (June 1925), 413—417.

Rahill, Frank. "Melodrama," *Theatre Arts Monthly* (N.Y.), XVI, No. 4 (April 1932), 285—294.

Roberts, Preston T. "A Christian Theory of Dramatic Tragedy," *Journal of Religion* (Chicago), XXXI (1951), 1—20.

-- "Bringing Pathos into Focus," *University of Chicago Magazine* (1954).

Santayana, George. "Tragic Philosophy," *Scrutiny; A Quarterly Review* (Cambridge), IV, No. 4 (March 1936), 365–376.

Scheler, Max. "On the Tragic," *Cross Currents* (Winter 1954). [This is a selection from Scheler's *Vom Umsturtz der Werte*, Vol. 1 (1923), trans. by Bernard Stambler].

Schwartz, Elias. "Detachment and Tragic Effect," *College English*, XVIII, No. 3 (December 1956), 153–156.

Sewall, Richard B. "The Tragic Form," *Essays in Criticism* (Oxford), IV, No. 4 (October 1954), 345–358.

Smart, John S. "Tragedy," *Essays and Studies* (Oxford), VIII (1922), 9–36.

Spivack, Charlotte K. "Tragedy and Comedy; A Metaphysical Wedding," *Bucknell Review*, IX (1960), 212–223.

Spoerri, Theophil. "Das Problem des Tragischen," *Trivium* (Zurich), V (1947), 153–179.

Stolnitz, Jerome. "Notes on Comedy and Tragedy," *Philosophy and Phenomenological Research* (Buffalo, N.Y.), XVI, No. 1 (September 1955), 45–60.

Stratman, Carl J. "Unpublished Dissertations in the History

and Theory of Tragedy, 1889–1957," *Bulletin of Bibliography*, XXII (1959), 237–240; XXIII (1960), 15–20.

Taubes, Susan. "The Nature of Tragedy," *Review of Metaphysics* (New Haven) (December 1953).

Walker, George. "On Tragedy and the Interest in Tragical Representatives," *Memoirs of the Manchester Literary and Philosophical Society*, V, pt. 2 (1798).

Wasserman, Earl R. "The Pleasures of Tragedy," *ELH* (Baltimore), XIV, No. 4 (December 1947), 283–307.

Watts, Harold H. "Myth and Drama," *Cross Currents* (1955)

DATE DUE

GAYLORD			PRINTED IN U.S.A.